EVERYTHING SPORTS

EVERYTHING BASEBALL

CORBU STATHES

SportsZone

An Imprint of Abdo Publishing
abdobooks.com

abdobooks.com

Printed in the United States of America, North Mankato, Minnesota.
052024
092024

THIS BOOK CONTAINS RECYCLED MATERIALS

Cover Photos: Ron Jenkins/Getty Images Sport/Getty Images, front (Corey Seager); David Berding/Getty Images Sport/Getty Images, front (Royce Lewis); Shutterstock Images, front (background), back
Interior Photos: Photo 12/Universal Images Group/Getty Images, 4–5; Bettmann/Getty Images, 7, 10–11; Ron Jenkins/Getty Images Sport/Getty Images, 8–9; Jed Jacobsohn/Getty Images Sport/Getty Images, 12–13; Mark Rucker/Transcendental Graphics/Getty Images Sport/Getty Images, 14–15, 32–33, 34–35; Sporting News/Getty Images, 16–17; Tony Dejak/AP Images, 19; Transcendental Graphics/Archive Photos/Getty Images, 20; David Durochik/AP Images, 21; Thearon W. Henderson/Getty Images Sport/Getty Images, 22–23; Jerry Hoefer/Fort Worth Star-Telegram/AP Images, 24–25; Patrick McDermott/Washington Nationals/Getty Images Sport/Getty Images, 26–27; James Drake/Getty Images Sport/Getty Images, 28–29; Focus on Sport/Getty Images, 30, 58; Rob Leiter/Major League Baseball/Getty Images, 31; Loren Elliott/Major League Baseball/Getty Images, 36–37; Nick Cammett/Diamond Images/Getty Images, 39; Jeffrey Brown/Icon Sportswire/Getty Images, 40; Al Bello/Getty Images Sport/Getty Images, 41; G. Fiume/Getty Images Sport/Getty Images, 42–43; Matt Slocum/AP Images, 44–45; Michael Ivins/Boston Red Sox/Getty Images Sport/Getty Images, 46–47; Warren Wimmer/Icon Sportswire/AP Images, 48–49; Frank Gunn/The Canadian Press/AP Images, 50; Rob Carr/Getty Images Sport/Getty Images, 51; Jay Biggerstaff/Getty Images Sport/Getty Images, 52–53; Tim Nwachukwu/Getty Images Sport/Getty Images, 55; Eric Espada/Getty Images Sport/Getty Images, 56–57; Otto Greule Jr./Getty Images Sport/Getty Images, 59; Wally Skalij/Los Angeles Times/Getty Images, 60–61

Editor: Charlie Beattie
Series Designer: Karli Kruse

Library of Congress Control Number: 2023949392
Publisher's Cataloging-in-Publication Data
Names: Stathes, Corbu, author.
Title: Everything baseball / by Corbu Stathes
Description: Minneapolis, Minnesota: Abdo Publishing, 2025 | Series: Everything sports | Includes online resources and index.
Identifiers: ISBN 9781098293550 (lib. bdg.) | ISBN 9798384912828 (ebook)
Subjects: LCSH: Baseball--Juvenile literature. | Baseball players--Juvenile literature. | Baseball coaches--Juvenile literature. | Baseball fields--Juvenile literature. | Baseball teams--Juvenile literature. | Baseball injuries--Juvenile literature. | Sports--Juvenile literature. | Baseball-History--Juvenile literature. | Baseball--Records--Juvenile literature. | Baseball programs--Juvenile literature.
Classification: DDC 796.357--dc23

TABLE OF CONTENTS

CHAPTER ONE

A STORIED HISTORY

Baseball began to take shape back in the mid-1800s. For many years, fans believed a former US Army soldier named Abner Doubleday invented the sport in 1839. This turned out not to be true. Instead, baseball slowly developed over time.

In 1845, Alexander J. Cartwright organized the New York Knickerbockers Base Ball Club. Cartwright also wrote down standard rules for the sport. It was from those rules that the modern game was born.

Early baseball teams were made up of amateur players. But in 1869, a man named Harry Wright put together the first professional team—the Cincinnati Red Stockings. Two years later, the National Association of Professional Base Ball Players formed. It included nine teams spread across Illinois, Indiana, Massachusetts, New York, Ohio, Pennsylvania, and Washington, DC. It lasted until 1876, when the National

The Elysian Fields in Hoboken, New Jersey, were some of the first baseball parks in the United States.

CINCINNATI RED STOCKINGS

The 1869 Cincinnati Red Stockings traveled across the country to take on the best local teams. The team's 10 players traveled on trains, steamboats, and stagecoaches on their coast-to-coast journey. Wherever the Red Stockings went, they drew huge crowds. They also always won. Cincinnati finished the season 57–0.

League (NL) was formed. By 1900, the NL had teams in Boston, Brooklyn, Chicago, Cincinnati, New York City, Philadelphia, Pittsburgh, and St. Louis.

The NL was mostly located in the eastern United States. The Western League formed in 1893. At that time, the actual American West didn't have many big cities. So the Western League stretched from the East only to the Midwest.

The two leagues were friendly until 1901. That year, the Western League, which was now known as the American League (AL), put clubs in Baltimore, Boston, Philadelphia, and Washington, DC. The two leagues began battling for fans as well as top players. In 1903, they decided to settle those differences on the field. The NL's Pittsburgh Pirates and AL's Boston Americans played the first World Series. The series was set up in a best-of-nine game format. Boston won it, 5–3.

Excited fans flood the field at the Huntington Avenue Ground in Boston before Game 3 of the 1903 World Series. When police couldn't remove them, the game was played with many spectators in the field of play.

In the first half of the 1900s, baseball was by far the country's most popular sport. Fans without major league teams nearby could watch any of the hundreds of minor league clubs spread across the country. Some of those teams had players working their way toward Major League Baseball (MLB). Others were independent teams. People all over the United States flocked to baseball.

CHAPTER TWO

THE LONG BALL

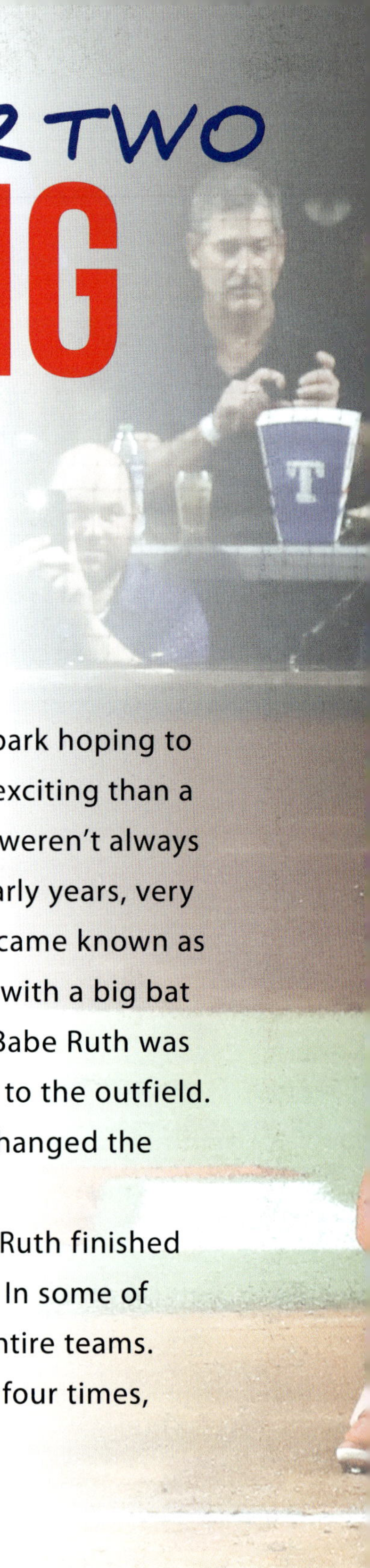

Today, many baseball fans head to the ballpark hoping to see a big home run. And nothing is more exciting than a walk-off blast over the fence. But home runs weren't always such a large part of baseball. In the sport's early years, very few balls sailed out of the park. That time became known as baseball's "dead-ball" era. In 1914, a big man with a big bat and even bigger personality arrived in MLB. Babe Ruth was originally a pitcher, but he eventually moved to the outfield. For 21 years, he hammered baseballs—and changed the sport along the way.

Playing mostly for the New York Yankees, Ruth finished his career with a then-record 714 home runs. In some of his early seasons, he hit more homers than entire teams. He broke the single-season home run record four times,

Aaron Judge of the New York Yankees launches his AL-record 62nd home run late in the 2022 season.

Babe Ruth broke the existing record of 138 career home runs in 1921, when he was still only 26 years old.

but his most famous season came in 1927. That year he hit 60 homers, a mark that stood for 34 years.

Ruth's most famous homer came in the 1932 World Series. The Yankees were in Chicago to face the Cubs in Game 3. In the fifth inning, Ruth came up to bat. Cubs players were jeering him from the dugout. In response, Ruth is said to have pointed his bat toward the outfield. He then walloped a home run to the spot where he supposedly pointed. To this day, baseball fans debate what really happened. Some are sure Ruth predicted his home run. Skeptics say Ruth was merely pointing to the hecklers in the Chicago dugout. No matter what really happened, Ruth's "called shot" still stands as one of baseball's most famous moments.

Neither of Ruth's home run records still stand. Another Yankee, Roger Maris, hit 61 homers in 1961. In 1998, two sluggers took aim at

WORLD SERIES WALK-OFFS

The walk-off home run is one of baseball's dramatic moments. It's even more exciting when a walk-off shot ends the World Series. It has only happened twice. In 1960, Bill Mazeroski of the Pittsburgh Pirates beat the New York Yankees 10–9 with a solo home run in the ninth inning of Game 7. In 1993, outfielder Joe Carter of the Toronto Blue Jays hit a three-run walk-off shot against the Philadelphia Phillies in Game 6. The 8–6 victory clinched a 4–2 series win for Toronto.

Maris's mark. Sammy Sosa of the Cubs and Mark McGwire of the St. Louis Cardinals thrilled fans all summer by chasing history. In the end, McGwire hit 70 home runs. Sosa finished with 66. But McGwire's mark stood for only three seasons. Barry Bonds of the San Francisco Giants socked 73 in 2001.

Ruth's career record of 714 home runs lasted longer. Some believed that it would never be matched. But on April 8, 1974, legendary outfielder Hank Aaron broke it by hitting his 715th home run. Aaron's eventual career mark of 755 lasted until 2007, when Bonds passed him. Bonds retired after that season. When he was finished, he had 762 career homers.

However, the new records were all controversial. Bonds, McGwire, and Sosa were all accused of using performance-enhancing drugs in their careers. The three players' statistics still stand. But many baseball fans and media members still hold up Ruth and Aaron as baseball's true home run icons.

Barry Bonds watches after connecting on his record-setting 71st home run of the 2001 season.

CHAPTER THREE

THE NEGRO LEAGUES

In the 1880s, racist MLB owners banned Black players from joining their clubs. But that did not stop Black men from making their mark on the national pastime. For years, Black teams barnstormed all over the country. They battled through fierce prejudice and segregation to play games wherever they could. In 1920, Rube Foster led the charge to organize a league. Foster was a former pitcher who had become manager and owner of the Chicago American Giants. Along with seven other teams, the American Giants helped form the Negro National League (NNL) that season. It was the first of many leagues for Black players.

For more than 30 years, the Negro Leagues turned out some of baseball's greatest players. Superstars such as outfielder James "Cool Papa" Bell, catcher Josh Gibson, and

Josh Gibson reportedly hit nearly 800 home runs in his 17-year Negro Leagues career.

THE AGELESS SATCHEL PAIGE

Satchel Paige officially pitched for nine Negro League teams. But on days off, the right-hander liked to barnstorm with other teams in a special jersey he had made. In 1948, Paige joined Cleveland in the American League and helped the team win the World Series. He was 42 years old at the time, but he pitched five more years. In 1965, at age 59, he joined the Kansas City Athletics for one game. Paige pitched three scoreless innings.

first baseman/outfielder Oscar Charleston played their entire careers in the Negro Leagues.

Jackie Robinson spent a season with the Kansas City Monarchs in 1945. Two years later he changed baseball forever by joining MLB's Brooklyn Dodgers. Other Negro League stars followed as MLB's racist policy against signing Black players eventually faded away. Players such as Hank Aaron, Ernie Banks, Larry Doby, Monte Irvin, and Willie Mays were some of the best MLB players of the 1950s and 1960s. All started their careers in the Negro Leagues.

The Negro Leagues didn't survive, as their best players left for MLB. But their legacy remains a huge part of baseball history. In 2020, MLB finally recognized the Negro Leagues as major leagues, meaning the players' statistics and records were considered the same as MLB numbers.

Jackie Robinson hit .375 for the Kansas City Monarchs in 1945, his only season in the Negro Leagues.

CHAPTER FOUR

RECORD SMASHERS

For a long time, the most important stats for hitters were batting average, home runs, and runs batted in (RBIs). If a player topped his league in all three of those categories during a single season, he was said to have won the Triple Crown. It has happened 28 times in MLB history. But only four of them have happened since 1956. That year, Mickey Mantle of the New York Yankees led all three categories. The next to achieve the feat was Frank Robinson of the Baltimore

A MAGICAL YEAR

The Summer of 1941 saw two amazing hitting feats. First, Joe DiMaggio of the New York Yankees recorded a hit in 56 straight games. Ted Williams also finished the year hitting .406. DiMaggio's record still stands. And while many players had hit .400 before Williams, no one has done it since. The closest challenger was Tony Gwynn, who hit .394 in 1994.

Orioles in 1966. A year later, outfielder Carl Yastrzemski of the Boston Red Sox did it. After that, no one won the Triple Crown again until Miguel Cabrera of the Detroit Tigers hit .330 with 44 home runs and 139 RBIs for the Detroit Tigers in 2012.

Only four players have won the Triple Crown more than once. Boston legend Ted Williams accomplished the feat in 1942 and 1947. Rogers Hornsby of the St. Louis Cardinals did it twice in the 1920s. Josh Gibson won Negro National League Triple Crowns in 1936 and 1937. But the king of

Miguel Cabrera of the Detroit Tigers watches a home run leave the ballpark.

the Triple Crown was another Negro Leagues star. Oscar Charleston did it three times—in 1921, 1924, and 1925.

Other players are revered for their ability to get on base. Detroit Tigers all-time great Ty Cobb retired in 1928 with 4,189 hits. That was more than 700 more than anyone else at the time. Cobb's record stood until September 11, 1985. That night, Pete Rose of the Cincinnati Reds knocked a single to

Oscar Charleston hit over .400 in all three of his Triple Crown seasons.

Rickey Henderson also holds the MLB record with 2,295 runs scored.

right field to pass Cobb's mark. Rose retired a year later with 4,256 hits.

Once on base, speedy players try to steal their way around the diamond. No one was a better thief than Rickey Henderson. Over a 25-year career with nine teams, the outfielder swiped 1,406 bases. That's 468 more than Lou Brock in second place. Henderson also set the single-season mark by stealing 130 in 1982.

CHAPTER FIVE

ON THE MOUND

Pitchers have their own ways to capture glory on the diamond. While some fans live for offense, others show up hoping to see pitchers dominate. The height of pitching is the perfect game. That's when a pitcher retires all 27 batters he faces in a nine-inning game. At one point, this rare feat didn't happen for 34 straight years.

The most famous pitching performance happened in the World Series. In 1956, Don Larsen, a journeyman pitcher for the New York Yankees, threw a perfect game in Game 5 of the Fall Classic against the Brooklyn Dodgers. Larsen struck out seven batters in a 2–0 win.

A small step down from the perfect game is the no-hitter. While a perfect game means 27 batters and 27 outs, a no-hitter is slightly different. A pitcher might allow

Domingo Germán of the New York Yankees threw the 24th perfect game in MLB history on June 28, 2023, against the Oakland Athletics.

baserunners through walks or errors in a no-hitter. But they still don't allow any base hits. The undisputed king of the no-hitter was fireballing right-hander Nolan Ryan. In his 27-year career, Ryan threw seven of them. His last came in 1991, when he was 44 years old.

In Game 4 of the 2022 World Series, four Houston Astros pitchers combined for a no-hitter against the Philadelphia Phillies. Cristian Javier, Bryan Abreu, Rafael Montero, and Ryan Pressly allowed only three walks in the game and struck out 14 batters. Houston won 5–0 on its way to a World Series title.

Another way pitchers can make their mark is by piling up strikeouts. On four occasions, pitchers have struck out 20 batters in a nine-inning game. Roger Clemens did it twice, 10 years apart, while playing for the Boston Red Sox. He fanned 20 Seattle Mariners in 1986. In 1996, Clemens struck out 20 Detroit Tigers. Kerry Wood struck out 20 Astros while playing for the Chicago Cubs in 1998. Wood allowed only one hit in

JOHNNY VANDER MEER

One of the most amazing feats ever pulled off in baseball came from pitcher Johnny Vander Meer in 1938. The Cincinnati Reds' lefty no-hit the Boston Bees on June 11. Four days later, he struck out seven Brooklyn Dodgers in a second straight no-hitter. Vander Meer is the only pitcher to ever throw two such games in a row.

Nolan Ryan salutes the crowd in Texas after throwing his seventh career no-hitter in 1991.

Max Scherzer winds up during his 20-strikeout performance against the Detroit Tigers on May 11, 2016.

a 2–0 victory. In May 2016, Max Scherzer of the Washington Nationals struck out 20 Detroit Tigers while winning 3–2.

The record for strikeouts in a game is 21. Tom Cheney of the Washington Senators reached that mark in a 2–1 win over the Baltimore Orioles on September 13, 1962. But Cheney's record comes with a catch: the game took 16 innings, and Cheney pitched all of them.

In baseball's early years, most pitchers threw all nine innings. But as baseball evolved, relief pitchers became an important part of any team. In 1969, relievers got their own key stat—the save. The king of the late innings is former Yankee Mariano Rivera. The star closer saved a record 652 games between 1995 and 2013. He also had 42 saves in the playoffs as he helped New York win five World Series.

CHAPTER SIX

AMAZING MOMENTS

Fans go to baseball games knowing they might see something amazing. In Game 1 of the 1954 World Series, Cleveland hitter Vic Wertz launched a long fly ball. It appeared well on its way to a huge hit. Instead, New York Giants center fielder Willie Mays sprinted with his back to home plate and made an over-the-shoulder catch just after his hat flew off. The amazing grab kept the game tied 2–2. New York went on to win that game and the series.

THE STREAK

On September 6, 1995, Cal Ripken Jr. of the Baltimore Orioles played his 2,131st consecutive game, a streak that started in 1982. With that, Ripken became baseball's "iron man." His streak broke the old mark set by Hall-of-Fame first baseman Lou Gehrig of the New York Yankees. Gehrig had played 2,130 straight games between 1925 and 1939. By the time Ripken took a rest in 1998, his streak had reached 2,632 games.

Willie Mays, *right*, is considered one of the most exciting players to ever suit up in the major leagues.

The iconic play has lived on in baseball lore. It has a simple nickname: "the Catch."

Other games, meanwhile, have turned on terrible mistakes. Entering the 1986 World Series, the Boston Red Sox hadn't won a championship since 1918. In the 10th inning of Game 6 against the New York Mets, Boston was within one out of breaking that curse. But the Red Sox blew the lead. The final play was a slow ground ball to first baseman Bill Buckner. The ball went through the veteran's legs, which allowed New York's winning run to score. No one forgot Buckner's error, especially after the Mets won Game 7 to take the series.

Ray Knight (22) scores the winning run in Game 6 of the 1986 World Series for the New York Mets after Bill Buckner's error.

Every year on April 15, all MLB players wear Jackie Robinson's No. 42 on their jerseys to honor the anniversary of Robinson's debut.

Baseball's most important moment came on April 15, 1947. That day, Jackie Robinson started at first base for the Brooklyn Dodgers. Robinson was the first Black player to take part in an NL or AL game for 60 years. For decades, team owners refused to sign Black players, no matter how talented.

Robinson battled through years of racist abuse but was a star on the field. He won MLB's first Rookie of the Year Award. In 1949, he was the NL's Most Valuable Player (MVP). Robinson also won the 1955 World Series with the Dodgers. He retired a year later having changed baseball forever. Today, his No. 42 jersey is retired by every team in the league.

CHAPTER SEVEN

WOMEN IN BASEBALL

Many people think of baseball as a men's sport. However, women have been playing baseball for nearly 200 years. Vassar College in New York formed a women's team in 1866. In 1898, Lizzie Arlington became the first woman to play for a professional men's team. But the league banned Arlington after just one game.

Women finally got a chance to showcase their skills in the 1940s. Many men, including MLB players, were overseas fighting in World War II (1939–45). Chicago Cubs owner Philip Wrigley decided to start a women's softball league. The players soon switched to baseball, and in 1943 the All-American Girls Professional Baseball League (AAGPBL) was born. The league started with four teams in Wisconsin,

Edythe Perlick of the Racine Belles takes a swing during an All-American Girls Professional Baseball League game in 1947.

Effa Manley used her position as a baseball owner to help fight for many civil rights causes.

Illinois, and Indiana. The Racine Belles won the first title 3–0 over the Kenosha Comets.

The league grew to 10 teams and featured more than 600 players before folding in 1954. The most successful season came in 1948, when more than 900,000 fans came out to see AAGPBL games. That year, the Rockford Peaches won one of their four league titles. No AAGPBL team won more.

Baseball opportunities since then have mostly been for boys and men. Girls and women, meanwhile, played softball instead. But many pioneering women have still found ways to make baseball history. In 1935, Effa Manley became co-owner of the Newark Eagles of the NNL, along with her husband, Abe. Effa was one of the league's fiercest promoters. She was also an excellent judge of talent. In 1946, the Eagles won the Negro World Series. Manley passed away in 1981.

MO'NE DAVIS

On August 15, 2014, 13-year-old Mo'Ne Davis took the mound for her Philadelphia-area team at the Little League World Series (LLWS). She pitched six innings and tossed eight strikeouts. Davis's team won 4–0. That made her the first girl to win a game in the storied tournament's history. Davis became a national celebrity for her baseball skill. She went on to play college softball at Hampton University in Virginia.

But in 2006, she became the first woman elected to the National Baseball Hall of Fame.

After years of making minor strides, women achieved many milestones in the 2010s and early 2020s. In 2015, Jessica Mendoza became the first woman to broadcast an MLB game for ESPN. The former softball star was in the booth for a game on August 24th between the St. Louis Cardinals and the Arizona Diamondbacks. Mendoza is still one of the network's top baseball announcers.

Before the 2020 season, Alyssa Nakken made history when she was hired as an assistant coach by the San Francisco Giants. That made her the first full-time female coach of an MLB team. Later that same year, Kim Ng became the first woman to be named general manager of an MLB team. Ng led the Miami Marlins to the playoffs twice in four seasons before leaving her post in 2023. Two days before Ng left her position, Nakken had interviewed to be the Giants' new manager. Though she did not get the job, her interview signaled that it might not be long before a woman managed at baseball's highest level.

Alyssa Nakken began working for the San Francisco Giants as an intern in 2014 before working her way up to the coaching staff.

CHAPTER EIGHT

THE MINOR LEAGUES

Almost every professional player spends time in baseball's minor leagues before he makes it to MLB. Some players spend years in the minors—and many of them never reach the big leagues. Every team has five minor league levels. They are labeled as Rookie, Low-A, High-A, Double-A, and the highest level, Triple-A.

NAME THAT TEAM

Some of the most interesting team nicknames in sports come from minor league baseball. Current teams include the Amarillo Sod Poodles in Texas, the Missoula Paddleheads in Montana, and the Rocket City Trash Pandas in Alabama. There were also once teams called the Holland Wooden Shoes, the Raleigh-Durham Triangles, and the Sweetwater Swatters.

The minor leagues are much more than a proving ground for new players. MLB often tries out potential new rules in minor league games.

Umpires, broadcasters, and team employees often start in the minors as well.

Attending a minor league baseball game can be a very different experience than going to an MLB game. Many minor league teams are well-known for the interesting ways they get fans to come to the ballpark. Some involve souvenir giveaways, special jerseys, or fireworks after the game. Others are much more creative. In 2012, a team in Montana started a new tradition called "Float to the Ballpark" night. A group of 75 fans arrive at the game after a two-hour

Jackson Holliday, *right*, of the Bowie Baysox tries to turn a double play against the Akron RubberDucks during a Double-A game in August 2023.

whitewater rafting trip down a nearby river. In 2016, a team in Pennsylvania challenged fans to run a full 26.2-mile (42.2-km) marathon in the time it took to play a game. The fans who competed ran laps around the ballpark.

The Savannah (Georgia) Bananas are an independent team. That means they don't work with an MLB club.

Team employees of the Louisville Bats greet fans on a Star Wars–themed night in May 2022.

Savannah Bananas owner Jesse Cole entertains the crowd during a 2023 game.

The Bananas have become famous for their on-field stunts. Their games have a special rule that allows batters to "steal" first base. They can also be called out if fans catch foul balls. Players are often seen doing choreographed dance routines between pitches. Another player hits and pitches while on stilts. The Bananas' games have come to be known as "Banana Ball." In 2023, the team drew more than 15,000 fans for one of its road contests.

CHAPTER NINE

SUPERSTITIONS AND CURSES

Baseball players can be a very superstitious bunch. If they're playing well, they might do odd things such as wear the same socks every day or get dressed the exact same way. Some players won't step on the foul lines when they go on or off the field. Others have a favorite hat, wristband, or shirt. Anything to keep luck on their side.

Individual players have had some strange superstitions over the years. Third baseman Wade Boggs ate chicken before every game. It seemed to work, as he retired in 1999 with 3,010 career hits. Slugger Larry Walker was obsessed with the number three. He wore No. 33 on his uniform, but he also set his morning alarm for 33 minutes past the hour. He was even married at 3:33 p.m.

Sometimes though, things happen that seem to bring an entire club bad luck. The Boston Red Sox won the World Series in 1918. But a year later, they sent star player

Members of the Washington Nationals flip their caps up during the late innings of a 2016 game. One baseball superstition says these "rally caps" will help a team score.

Babe Ruth to their fierce rivals, the New York Yankees. New York became the best team in baseball. Ruth won four titles in New York and helped the Yankees build baseball's greatest dynasty. Meanwhile, Boston didn't win another World Series for 85 years. The slump became known as the "Curse of the Bambino," after one of Ruth's nicknames.

However, no team suffered a longer stretch of pain than the Chicago Cubs. After winning the World Series in 1908, Chicago didn't do it again for more than a century. And that streak came with its own curse. When the Cubs reached the World Series in 1945, a local bar owner named William Sianis tried to bring his pet goat to one of the games. When Sianis and the goat were removed from the park, Sianis "cursed" the team. He said the Cubs would never win the World Series. He was right—until the Cubs rallied to win the 2016 Fall Classic against Cleveland and end 108 years of misery.

DON'T SAY IT

One of baseball's more interesting superstitions comes up during potential no-hitters. Many players believe in an unwritten rule that no one should talk about a no-hit bid while it is going on. They are forbidden to talk to the pitcher, or even say the word "no-hitter" on the bench. Many television and radio broadcasters also stick to this rule until the no-hitter is finished. They fear that mentioning it will jinx the pitcher into giving up a hit.

The Chicago Cubs celebrate after finally breaking the team's 108-year championship drought in 2016.

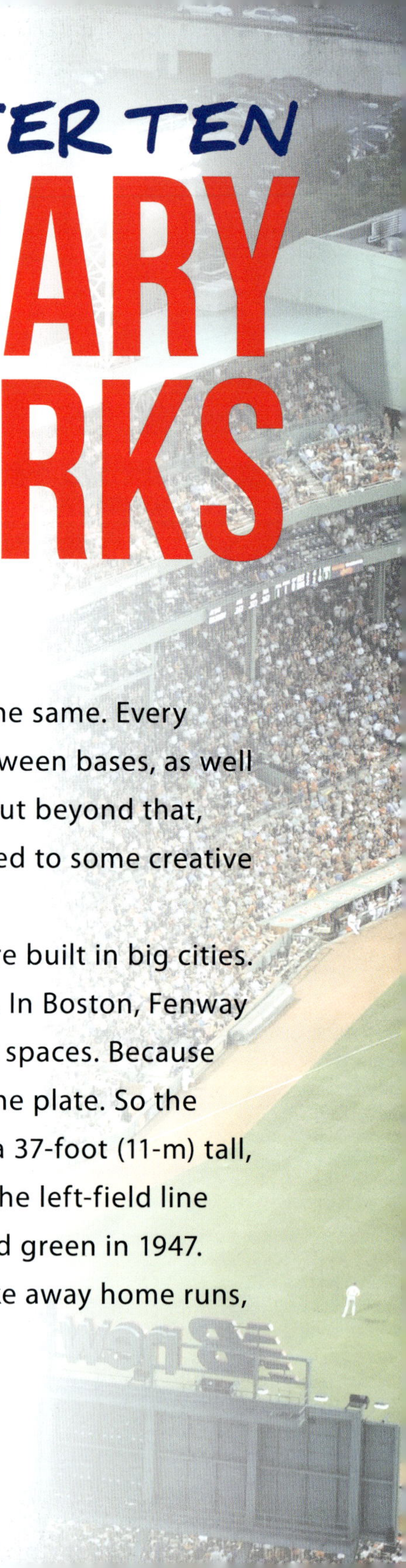

CHAPTER TEN

LEGENDARY BALLPARKS

A basic baseball diamond always looks the same. Every field uses the same measurements between bases, as well as between the mound and home plate. But beyond that, every ballpark can be different. That has led to some creative designs over the years.

In the beginning, all MLB ballparks were built in big cities. Sometimes that didn't leave a lot of room. In Boston, Fenway Park was squeezed into one of these tight spaces. Because of that, the left field wall was close to home plate. So the team decided to build up. The result was a 37-foot (11-m) tall, 231-foot (70-m) long fence running from the left-field line to nearly center field. The wall was painted green in 1947. Because of its size, color, and ability to take away home runs, it became known as the "Green Monster."

Built in 1912, Fenway Park in Boston is the oldest stadium in the majors.

Wrigley Field in Chicago is another ballpark built right into a neighborhood. Across the street from the outfield sit several apartment buildings. Fans used to be able to stand on the rooftops and watch the games for free. Wrigley Field's other odd quirk is its brick outfield fence. Instead of padding it, the groundskeepers grow ivy plants over the wall every summer.

In 1962, MLB added a team in Houston. Because of the terrible Texas summer heat, the team decided to play its games indoors. In 1965, the team moved into the Astrodome, an indoor stadium with real grass. The grass soon died from lack of sunlight, so the Astros needed a new solution. They decided to install artificial grass. Because of the team's nickname, it became known as AstroTurf. Soon, many other teams installed artificial turf in their stadiums.

HOME FIELD ADVANTAGE

A team can customize its home field in many ways to gain an advantage. Sometimes, when playing against speedy base stealers, a team will water the infield so much that it becomes a soggy mess that is hard to run on. Other teams have let the grass grow to slow down ground balls. "One of the best relationships you need to have is with your home groundskeeper," said longtime manager Buck Showalter. "There are a lot of things teams try to do to accentuate their strengths and minimize their weaknesses."

Los Angeles Dodgers outfielder Enrique Hernández battles the Ivy on the fence at Chicago's Wrigley Field as he searches for the ball.

Rogers Centre in Toronto is one of seven current MLB stadiums to have a retractable roof.

Many teams built indoor stadiums, but the Toronto Blue Jays went one step further in 1989. They built a retractable roof over their home park, SkyDome, which is now known as Rogers Centre. The roof can be closed on rainy or cold days, allowing the games to still be played in bad weather. But fans can enjoy bright sunshine on nice summer days.

Most of the ballparks in the 1960s, 1970s, and 1980s weren't very inspiring. Many were drab stadiums that baseball teams shared with local professional football teams. That began to change in the early 1990s. In 1992, the Baltimore Orioles opened Oriole Park at Camden Yards. It was designed to look like a baseball park from the early 1900s. Soon, every team wanted its own "retro" park. Between 1992 and 2020, 19 of MLB's 30 teams built new stadiums. Most copied some of the Orioles' original ideas. And almost all of them were built using natural grass.

Many modern ballparks, such as Oriole Park at Camden Yards in Baltimore, have been built in the downtown areas of their home cities.

CHAPTER ELEVEN

AMATEUR BASEBALL

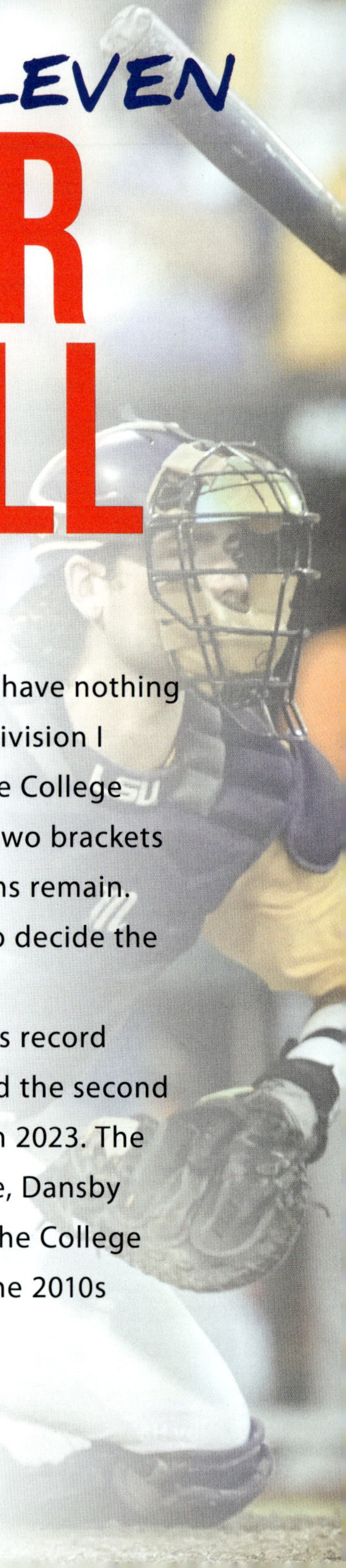

Two of the biggest baseball events each year have nothing to do with MLB. Every June, the best eight Division I college teams meet in Omaha, Nebraska, for the College World Series (CWS). The teams are placed into two brackets and play elimination games until only two teams remain. They then square off in a best-of-three series to decide the college national champion.

The University of Southern California won its record 12th title in 1998. Louisiana State University had the second most after winning its seventh championship in 2023. The tournament is never short on talent. Gerrit Cole, Dansby Swanson, and Adley Rutschman all went from the College World Series to eventually star in MLB during the 2010s and 2020s.

Colby Halter of the University of Florida follows through on a swing in a game against Louisiana State University during the 2023 College World Series.

In August, the baseball world focuses its attention on the small town of Williamsport, Pennsylvania. Williamsport has hosted the Little League World Series (LLWS) since 1947. Little League teams are made up of players 10 to 12 years old. In the early years, only a few states had teams. But the program quickly spread around the country and the world. Now there are teams in all 50 states, as well as in 80 other countries.

Each year, the best team from the United States faces the best team from the international tournament in a one-game championship. Through the first 76 tournaments, the American teams had a 39–37 edge in the series.

WORLD SERIES TRIFECTA

Only three players have appeared in the LLWS, the CWS, and the MLB World Series. Pitcher Ed Vosberg played for a team from Tucson, Arizona, in the LLWS; the University of Arizona in the CWS; and the Florida Marlins in the MLB World Series. Catcher Jason Varitek did the same for Almonte Springs, Florida; Georgia Tech University; and the Boston Red Sox. Outfielder Michael Conforto competed for Redmond, Oregon; Oregon State University; and the New York Mets. Conforto is also the only player to homer in all three events.

Max Baker of El Segundo, California, celebrates hitting a triple in the championship game of the 2023 Little League World Series.

CHAPTER TWELVE

BASEBALL AROUND THE WORLD

WORLD BASEBALL CLASSIC

The World Baseball Classic began play in 2006 with 16 countries participating. Japan won the first tournament. It repeated as champion in 2009. The Dominican Republic won in 2013, and the United States won its first title in 2017. Due to the COVID-19 pandemic, the tournament wasn't held again until 2023. Japan won again in an epic finish. Japan pitcher Shohei Ohtani struck out his Los Angeles Angels teammate Mike Trout of Team USA to end the championship game.

Baseball started in the United States, and it's become known as America's pastime. Along the way, the sport has spread around the world. People in approximately 80 countries play baseball, and several of those countries have professional leagues. Australia, the Dominican Republic, Mexico, and Venezuela have leagues that play during the

Venezuelan star Luis Arráez hits a home run during the 2023 World Baseball Classic. Arráez plays in MLB for the Miami Marlins.

Japanese legend Sadaharu Oh bats against the Los Angeles Dodgers in an exhibition game during the 1970s.

MLB off-season. These winter leagues are wildly popular with local fans. Many MLB players have played in these countries during their own off-season.

Japan's Nippon Professional Baseball League has a long, storied history. Legendary slugger Sadaharu Oh hit

868 home runs in Japan mostly in the 1960s and 1970s. Oh never played in MLB, but beginning in the 1990s, several Japanese stars crossed the Pacific Ocean to play in America.

Two of the most exciting players of the 2000s began their careers in Japan. Ichiro Suzuki was a sensation from

Ichiro Suzuki became the first Japanese position player to join an MLB team.

the moment he stepped on an MLB field in 2001. Playing for the Seattle Mariners, he led the league in hits. A swarm of Japanese reporters followed him everywhere and watched him win the AL Rookie of the Year and Most Valuable Player awards. Ichiro had more than 200 hits every year through 2010. In that span, he led the AL in hits six more times while also thrilling fans with his speed and rocket arm from right field.

When he finally left MLB in 2019, Ichiro had 3,089 hits. But he didn't start playing in MLB until he was 27. He also had more than 1,200 hits in nine seasons playing for the Orix Blue Wave in Japan.

Shohei Ohtani had been a slugger for the Nippon Ham Fighters in Japan for five seasons before joining the Los Angeles Angels in 2018. Like Ichiro, "Sho-Time" was an MLB star right away. He hit 22 home runs his first season with the Angels and was named AL Rookie of the Year. In his first six MLB seasons, Ohtani swatted 171 homers.

Hitting is only half of Ohtani's story. He is also one of the best pitchers in MLB. In 2022, he went 15–9 with a 2.33 earned-run average and 219 strikeouts. His dual-threat skills eventually earned him the largest contract in MLB history. In December 2023, Ohtani signed a 10-year, $700 million deal with the Los Angeles Dodgers.

Shohei Ohtani signed the largest contract in US sports history when he joined the Los Angeles Dodgers in 2023.

GLOSSARY

amateur
A person who plays a sport without getting paid.

barnstorm
To travel from place to place putting on performances or games.

groundskeeper
A person who takes care of a sports field.

journeyman
A player who has played for many teams or has been unable to find a specific role.

professional
A person who gets paid to perform.

racist
Discriminatory based on race.

rookie
An athlete in his or her first year of professional competition.

save
A stat awarded to a relief pitcher when he or she finishes a close game and secures a win.

segregation
The separation of groups of people based on race, gender, ethnicity, or other factors.

superstitious
Believing that unnatural forces have an impact on a person's actions.

veteran
A player who has played for many years.

walk-off
A victory in which the home team scores the winning run in the bottom of the final inning.

MORE INFORMATION

Books

Clarke, David J. *Baseball Strategies*. Abdo Publishing, 2024.

Hewson, Anthony K. *GOATs of Baseball*. Abdo Publishing, 2022.

Martin, Andrew. *Baseball's Greatest Players*. Rockridge Press, 2022.

Online Resources

Booklinks
NONFICTION NETWORK
FREE! ONLINE NONFICTION RESOURCES

To learn more about baseball, please visit **abdobooklinks.com** or scan this QR code. These links are routinely monitored and updated to provide the most current information available.

INDEX

About the Author

Corbu Stathes lives in Minnesota with his son. He works in college sports and loves researching and learning about new things.